HOW THEY LIVED

A SUFFRAGETTE

ANN KRAMER

Illustrated by
Steve Gibson

Wayland

HOW THEY LIVED

An American Pioneer Family
An Australian Pioneer
An Aztec Warrior
A Celtic Family
A Child in Victorian London
A Colonial American Merchant
A Crusading Knight
An Edwardian Household
A Family in the Fifties
A Family in the Thirties
A Family in World War I
A Family in World War II
An Ice Age Hunter
An Inca Farmer
A Medieval Monk
A Medieval Serf
A Norman Baron

A Plains Indian Warrior
A Plantation Slave
A Roman Centurion
A Roman Gladiator
A Sailor with Captain Cook
A Samurai Warrior
A Saxon Farmer
A Schoolchild in World War II
A Slave in Ancient Greece
A Soldier in Wellington's Army
A Soldier in World War I
A Suffragette
A Teenager in the Sixties
A Tudor Merchant
A Victorian Factory Worker
A Viking Sailor

Editor: Amanda Earl

First published in 1988 by
Wayland (Publishers) Limited
61 Western Road, Hove
East Sussex BN3 1JD, England

© Copyright 1988 Wayland (Publishers) Limited

All the words that appear in **bold** in the text are explained in the glossary on page 31.

British Library Cataloguing in Publication Data
Kramer, Ann
A Suffragette
1. Great Britain. Women's Suffrage Movements, to 1918
I. Title   II. Series
324.6′23′0941

ISBN 1 85210 203 9

Typeset by Kalligraphics Limited, Redhill, Surrey.
Printed and bound in Belgium by Casterman S.A.

CONTENTS

'VOTES FOR WOMEN' 4

PARLIAMENT AND THE VOTE 6

THE MAKING OF A SUFFRAGETTE 8

TACTICS 10

MEETINGS AND MARCHES 12

PRISON 14

MARRIAGE 16

LIFE AT HOME 18

WORK 20

CLOTHES AND APPEARANCE 22

HEALTH AND SICKNESS 24

RECREATION 26

WOMEN AT WAR 28

THE VOTE WON! 30

GLOSSARY 31

MORE BOOKS TO READ 31

INDEX 32

'VOTES FOR WOMEN'

The hall was hot and full to overflowing. On the platform a well-dressed man spoke in glowing terms of the great changes he would make if he were **elected** to Parliament. As he finished speaking, the audience clapped and cheered.

Two women sat just a row from the front. They were dressed in long, dark skirts with hats shielding their faces. Suddenly, the two women rose to their feet. Bravely they held up a small, white cotton banner bearing the words 'Votes for Women' in black lettering. In a low, but clear voice, one of the women called out, "Will a **Liberal government** give women the vote?".

Suddenly the hall was in uproar. Angry shouts filled the air, "Be quiet", "Sit down", "Throw those women out". Men at the sides of the

Two suffragettes disturb a public meeting to ask whether the Liberal government will give women the vote.

hall rushed towards the women. They disappeared into a sea of men and waving arms. Pushed and pulled, their clothes torn, their banner trampled, the two women were dragged out of the hall and thrown into the street, where they were taken away by the police.

The year was 1905. The two women were **suffragettes** – the brave and courageous women, dedicated to the cause of votes for women. From 1905 to 1914 they were the most famous women in Britain. Their activities filled the British press and shocked the British public. This book will tell you about their lives, the hardships they suffered and the excitement they experienced in the long, hard struggle for the vote.

Above *The suffragettes' motif, designed by Sylvia Pankhurst, was printed on many books and pamphlets.*

PARLIAMENT AND THE VOTE

In 1905, like today, Britain was governed by **Parliament**. Every five years people voted in general elections to choose representatives or Members of Parliament (MPs) who would make the laws and govern the country. But unlike today, women were not allowed to vote. Nor were there any women MPs.

During the nineteenth century, three Acts of Parliament had given the vote to most men. As the picture on this page shows, men who had been criminals, or of 'unsound mind' could still vote. Women, however, could be wives and mothers; they could be nurses, teachers and factory inspectors, but they did not have the right to vote.

Right *An anti-suffrage postcard, showing suffragettes battling with a policeman outside Parliament.*
Below *A leaflet handed out by suffragettes to persuade politicians that women should be able to vote.*

Most politicians believed that a woman's place was in the home, not on street corners demonstrating.

Throughout the nineteenth century, more and more women had been asking for the vote. Such women were known as **suffragists**, which comes from the word 'suffrage', meaning 'right to vote'. They believed that women, like men, should be able to help in deciding the laws of the country. However, they must not be confused with the suffragettes, who formed in the early twentieth century.

Many of the early suffragists, were middle class, educated women who were nervous of standing up in public and making their demands. They formed suffrage societies, held meetings, and petitioned Parliament, using respectable methods to try and persuade the government.

From 1867, men too began to talk about votes for women in the **House of Commons**. But each time Parliament refused to give women the vote. Most MPs believed that a woman's place was in the home. They believed that politics was a man's world and that women should have no part of it. Even Victoria, who was Queen of Britain from 1837–1901, was opposed to women having the vote!

This cartoon from Punch *magazine, shows the 1871 Women's Suffrage Bill being thrown out of Parliament.*

7

THE MAKING OF A SUFFRAGETTE

In 1903, a new suffrage society was formed called the Women's Social and Political Union (WSPU). It was started by a small group of determined women in Manchester, but within a few years had attracted thousands of women throughout the country and had opened offices in Clements Inn, London.

Unlike the suffragists, followers of the WSPU did not believe in using respectable methods to gain the vote. Led by two remarkable women, Mrs Emmeline Pankhurst and her daughter Christabel, the Union was very

The general offices of the Women's Social and Political Union in London.

Above *The WSPU was led by Emmeline Pankhurst (left) and her daughter Christabel. It was a very well organized union.*

Suffragettes outside one of the London branches of the WSPU.

well organized, and run like a volunteer army. Its members were prepared to use any means to get votes for women . . . even to break the law.

The followers of the Union were rebels, going against the **conventions** of the time. They soon became famous and, in 1906, were nicknamed 'suffragettes' by the *Daily Mail* newspaper. The word was first used as an insult to make fun of their unladylike behaviour, but the suffragettes were proud of the title and the name has stuck ever since.

The suffragettes came from all walks of life. Most came from the educated and well-to-do classes but there were also working-class women. They included mill workers from the north of England, factory workers and poor women from the East End of London. Teachers, office workers, actresses, clerks, **peeresses**, university students, married and unmarried women flocked to join the WSPU and to give their time, money and devotion to the 'cause', as the fight for the vote became known.

Tactics

The suffragettes were 'militants'. Militant means 'engaged in warfare'. Unlike suffragists who were prepared to work with Parliament, the suffragettes were determined to wage war on the government.

In 1905 they began a policy of heckling – interrupting speakers at public meetings, like the one at the beginning of this book. The first time this happened two suffragettes, Christabel Pankhurst and Annie Kenney, were arrested. The next day the newspapers were full of the story and votes for women was news.

The Liberal Party formed the government in 1906 and 1910, but refused to give women the vote. Heckling continued and soon suffragettes were banned from political meetings. But the daring women found ways to attend. Some dressed in disguise; others hid in halls before meetings.

On one occasion a massive meeting was interrupted by two suffragettes who had hidden all night in an organ before shouting, "votes for women", into the hall. At another meeting a suffragette was lowered down through a skylight in the ceiling. The brave woman had hidden in the ceiling for seventeen hours.

The suffragettes made their presence felt everywhere. They organized marches to Downing Street, home of the Liberal Prime Minister, Mr Asquith. Battles between the suffragettes and police were common and very violent. Some women chained themselves to

1908: A suffragette is thrown out of a political meeting after heckling the speaker.

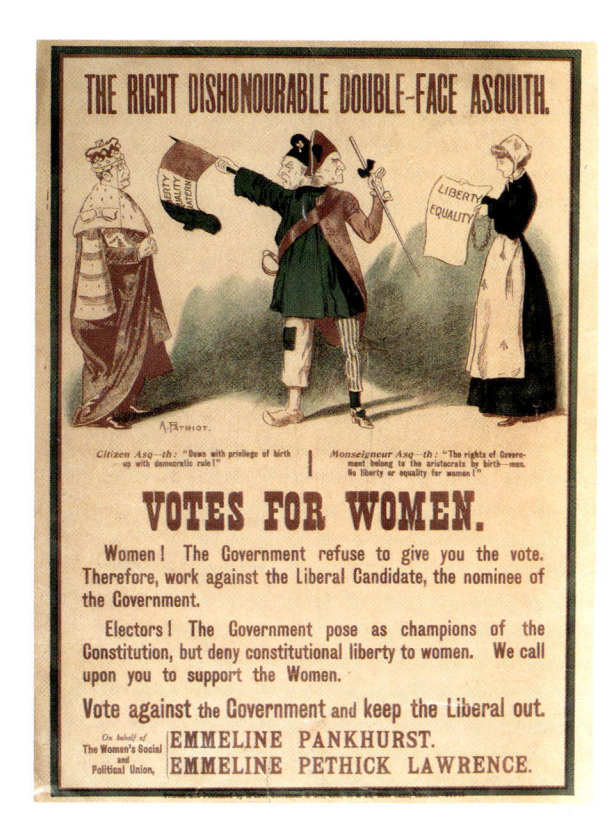

Left *A poster urging electors to vote against the Liberal Prime Minister, Mr Asquith.*

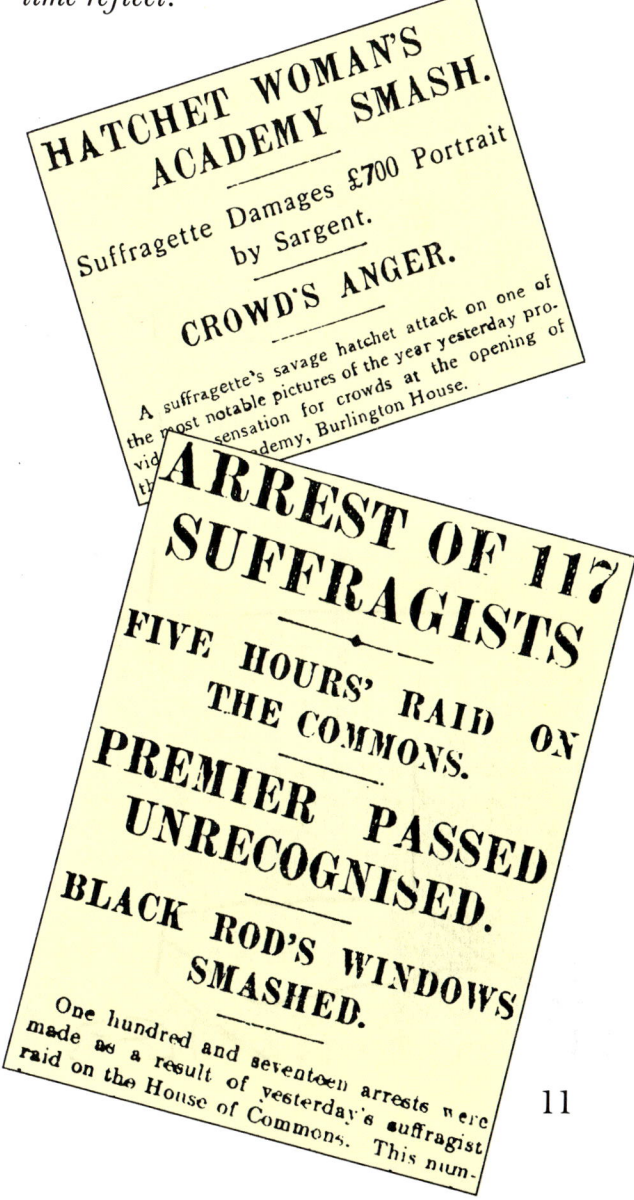

Below *From 1911, the tactics used by the suffragettes became more daring and radical, as these newspaper cuttings of the time reflect.*

railings to prevent the police from dragging them away.

Tactics such as these gave the suffragettes more publicity than any other suffrage society. The newspapers were full of their actions.

From 1911 the suffragettes began to use more dramatic tactics. They smashed hundreds of windows, bombed and set fire to houses, railway stations and other buildings. This lost them much support. But the suffragettes were not hooligans. They attacked property not people.

MEETINGS AND MARCHES

Suffragettes were always finding ways to draw attention to their cause. They produced a newspaper called *Votes for Women* and sold it on street corners. They also held meetings and made speeches. Some meetings were small. A suffragette would stand on a **soap box** at a street corner and talk to any passers by. It was a daring thing to do. Sometimes the audience was friendly. On other occasions suffragettes were hit with tomatoes, eggs or even stones, but they became used to insults.

Other meetings were much larger. In 1906, suffragettes held a meeting in London's Trafalgar Square. Eight thousand people came to hear the suffragettes speak.

Below *1908: Christabel Pankhurst (left) joins the first great suffragette rally in Hyde Park.*

Above *A suffragette selling the 'Votes for Women' newspaper.*

Suffragettes also organized marches and rallies. These were often dramatic affairs, full of colour, pageantry, and pride.

In 1908, the suffragettes held their first great rally in Hyde Park. Suffragettes were asked to wear the new WSPU colours – white for purity, green for hope, and purple for dignity. Thirty special trains brought women into London from 70 different cities. Seven separate **processions** made their way to Hyde Park

Trafalgar Square, 1906: Eight thousand people came to hear leading suffragettes speak.

where twenty platforms were set up for speakers. Marching women carried 700 purple, white and green banners.

The newspapers of the day estimated that as many as 500,000 people were in Hyde Park. For the suffragettes, it was a marvellous, thrilling occasion.

PRISON

Between 1906 and 1914 more than 1,000 suffragettes went to prison, and thousands were arrested for causing a nuisance. By 1911 Holloway Prison in London was so full of suffragettes that they formed a choir.

In prison a suffragette was dressed in rough prison clothes and put into a tiny cell. In her cell was one stool and a bed made of a plank of wood. Food consisted of gruel (a thin soup) and bread. For a middle-class woman prison was a harsh contrast to home.

Sentences were often long but prison was only a first step. In 1909 suffragettes began to go on hunger strikes as a protest because they were not treated as **political prisoners**. Some went without food for weeks until they were weak and faint.

Imprisonment was a terrifying experience for suffragettes. Their tiny cells only had a small bed, and they were dressed in rough prison clothes.

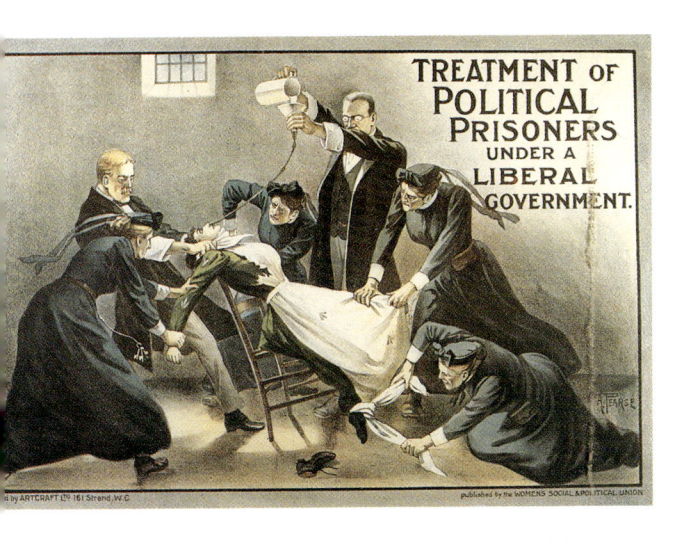

Above *Suffragettes were tortured by force feeding if they went on hunger strike.*

Worried that the women would starve themselves to death to become **martyrs**, the government introduced force feeding. It was a dreadful experience. The starving suffragette was held down, her mouth forced open and a rubber tube pushed through her mouth or nose into her stomach. Liquid food was poured down the tube. The tube was pulled out roughly and the suffragette was left bleeding and in pain until the next time.

Force feeding was torture. A woman in her cell could hear other suffragettes screaming as they were fed. Only young strong women could survive such treatment. But a suffragette had great physical courage and many returned time and time again to prison.

In 1913, force feeding ended. The government introduced what was known as the 'Cat and Mouse Act'. Starving women were released from prison and then rearrested when they were well again.

Below *A suffragette poster condemning the Liberal government's 'Cat and Mouse Act' of 1913.*

MARRIAGE

Most of the suffragettes were unmarried women or 'spinsters' as they were sometimes called then. A few were widows whose husbands had died. It was certainly easier for unmarried women to become involved in the work of the WSPU.

By the early part of the twentieth

Below *Traditionally, it was believed that a woman's place was in the home, caring for the children. Women were usually financially dependent on men.*

Above *Suffragettes wanted independence and equality with men. This cartoon shows a 'modern girl', with her worried parents looking on.*

century there were more **opportunities** for unmarried women than for married women. Even so, marriage was still considered to be the most desirable goal for women. Yet,

A group of suffragette supporters. Not all men were against women's suffrage.

however desirable it was, there were still disadvantages to being married. A married woman was supposed to be completely **dependent** on her husband. Before 1870 married woman were not allowed to own property. They were not supposed to earn their own living, and married women could not even apply for some jobs.

One of the popular arguments against giving women the vote was that it would threaten family life and even early suffragists were against giving married women the vote.

By their actions married suffragettes challenged these views. They believed in married women having **independence**. They wanted equality in marriage. Fortunately some of these suffragettes had sympathetic husbands who gave them support and encouragement, but their support was not always straightforward. The husband of one working-class suffragette, Hannah Mitchell, paid her fine to release her from prison. Hannah was furious and often wondered if her husband was more interested in her preparing his tea than votes for women!

LIFE AT HOME

The home life of a suffragette varied according to her class. Wealthy suffragettes usually came from large, comfortable homes with many rooms. They had servants to cook meals, clean the house as well as look after the children, if the woman was married.

Poorer suffragettes, by contrast, came from smaller homes, perhaps one of a row of terraced houses. Most

Below *Life for suffragettes differed, depending on their class. Poorer suffragettes, such as mill workers, came from homes like these.*

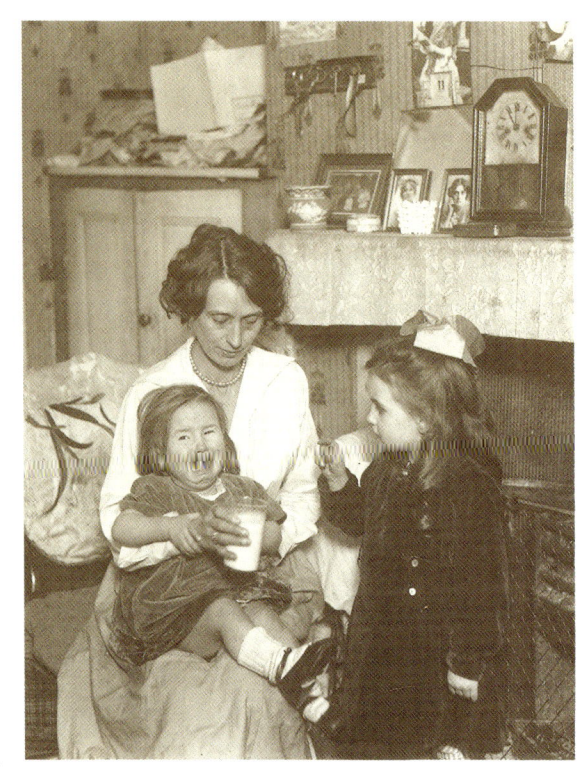

Above *Working-class suffragettes had no servants to help them, and often had to work as well as tend to a family.*

worked outside the home and also did all the work at home. There was a lot of work to do – cleaning, washing, cooking, mending as well as caring for the children and husband.

Some of the suffragettes came from families whose parents were involved

A suffragette march in Dundee, Scotland. Poorer suffragettes could not afford to be arrested too often.

in politics. The wealthier suffragettes, such as the leaders of the movement, were used to the hustle and bustle of politics and knew many of the leading political figures. Some working-class suffragettes too came from political backgrounds, their fathers or themselves having been active in **trade unions**.

For working-class women it was difficult to be militant. Not many working-class women could afford to lose their job through imprisonment. Some did go to prison, but to do so they had to prepare well in advance. Before leaving for a rally or demonstration the house was cleaned, meals were prepared and arrangements were made with relatives or neighbours to look after the children.

WORK

Although it was said that a woman's place was in the home, many of the suffragettes worked outside.

Women worked in the cotton mills, leaving home at 5 am to start work at 6 am. They worked an 11½-hour day. Other working-class women were factory workers or dressmakers working 10½ hours a day for as little as 8 shillings (40p).

Below *Many suffragettes also worked outside the home in factories and mills. Working hours were very long.*

Above *Suffragette Annie Kenney, a cotton-mill worker from Oldham, pictured in Manchester Jail.*

Opportunities for middle-class women had opened up in the years before the WSPU began. Women now worked as school teachers or nurses, professions into which they had only recently been accepted.

Women worked in other areas too – as shop workers, secretaries, clerks and typists. These occupations for women were created by **industrialization** and the growth of technology.

In all work however, women were paid far less than men. Some earned only half of a man's wage or sometimes two-thirds. They were also

Below *Job opportunities did improve at the beginning of this century. Work in offices as secretaries or telephonists was popular.*

In 1906, Christabel Pankhurst passed her law degree, but women could not become lawyers. It was not until 1922, that the first woman was accepted as a lawyer.

barred from the higher professional jobs. Women could not be bankers, lawyers or judges. Nor were they allowed into skilled work, such as engineering. For many of the suffragettes, the vote represented a way of improving this situation.

CLOTHES AND APPEARANCE

Clothes and appearance were important to the suffragettes. They took great care over what they wore and how they dressed. Many of them dressed in very traditional 'feminine' clothes. They wanted to show that, despite all the insults thrown at them, they were not 'man-like' women.

For marches, suffragettes dressed as well as they could afford. The WSPU colours were white for purity, green for hope, and purple for dignity.

To prove their point, suffragettes that could afford to, dressed in all the stylish clothes of the time. They wore silk dresses, trimmed with lace and long flowing scarves. They wore large-brimmed hats and their hair was swept up into place.

None of these clothes were practical. Most marches and demonstrations ended in violent scuffles with the police. The women's clothes were frequently torn and they emerged totally dishevelled.

To protect themselves from blows and injury some suffragettes stuffed cardboard under their clothes. After a demonstration they removed their clothes and a fine brown dust would shower the floor. Mackintoshes or raincoats were also worn if suffragettes were speaking on a street corner. It provided protection against any eggs or tomatoes that might be thrown!

The suffragettes enjoyed dressing up, particularly for demonstrations. The WSPU colours of purple, white and green could be seen everywhere. Sometimes suffragettes wore costumes – they dressed up as Joan of Arc, Queen Elizabeth I, Lady Godiva, or other female heroines of the past. It was all good publicity!

Suffragettes often wore 'feminine', lacy clothes, to disprove comments that they were 'man-like women'.

Some suffragettes started to wear loose, baggy trousers. This postcard makes fun of such fashions.

23

HEALTH AND SICKNESS

Life was exhausting for an active militant suffragette. There were meetings to organize, halls to book, money to raise, leaflets to print and **canvassing**. All this had to be done under the ever-present threat of being thrown into prison.

Hunger strikes and force feeding sometimes damaged women's health for life. Women came out of prison thin and weak. Some even suffered injuries to their lungs or stomach. Most women were nursed back to health at the WSPU's private house. After the 'Cat and Mouse

Below *Sylvia Pankhurst, daughter of Emmeline, talks at a public meeting. Life for a suffragette was exhausting.*

Above *Regular terms in prison took their toll on a suffragette's health.*

Act', the house became known as 'Mouse Castle' because so many 'mice', or released suffragettes, went there to recover or hide from the police.

Some women, particularly older women became permanent invalids.

Scrolls such as this one, were given to suffragettes who had been in prison.

One upper-class woman, who had disguised herself in order to experience the horrors of force feeding herself, told no one else she had a weak heart. On her release from prison she became seriously ill, suffered a stroke, and remained an invalid until her death.

Battles with the police took their toll too. After one particularly violent skirmish, known as 'Black Friday', 50 suffragettes suffered serious injuries that took weeks to heal. They had been kicked, their arms twisted, and their breasts punched.

Some suffragettes suffered depression and nervous breakdowns caused by the brutality and years of struggle. But the majority were young, strong women. The excitement and activity kept them going, and the years of the cause were remembered as the most exciting of their lives.

Below *The Suffragette magazine reports the death of Emily Davison, who sacrificed her life for the cause. She threw herself under the King's horse at the Epsom Derby in 1913.*

RECREATION

Being a suffragette did not leave much spare time. Those who were most active in the WSPU were expected to devote their entire time to the cause and nothing else. They were not supposed to go to concerts, the theatre, to smoke or to become involved in other activities.

Despite the discipline of the WSPU, life for a suffragette did have its lighter side. Weekly 'At Homes' were held at the Clements Inn headquarters and many women came. Tea was served and women sat in the offices talking and discussing the issues of the day.

Suffragettes often enjoyed a day at their headquarters, where they talked and relaxed over tea.

Suffragettes sometimes dressed up as famous heroines from history. It was good fun and good publicity.

Walking was a popular pastime; many of the suffragettes took long walks in the country. In their homes women sat around the fire talking about politics, making plans and remembering events. Sometimes they rehearsed the best methods of heckling. One woman pretended to be a leading political figure while the others heckled. This type of activity always caused much laughter.

Cycling was popular too, and many suffragettes also enjoyed reading and listening to music. The Union formed its own fife and drum band which played at many demonstrations, and among the suffragettes there were musicians, artists and actresses. Songs like *March of the Women* were composed and sung on marches and even in prison.

Above all women enjoyed the friendship of being with other women who passionately held the same beliefs as themselves.

Medals were awarded to many suffragettes who helped fight for the cause.

WOMEN AT WAR

The First World War began in 1914, and continued until 1918. With the outbreak of war the militant suffragette movement came to an end. Mrs Pankhurst called for a **truce** and urged the suffragettes to work with the government in the war against Germany. Some suffragettes were shocked at these instructions, and not all agreed. Some joined the peace movement against the war; others continued to work for suffrage in a peaceful way. By 1917 the WSPU no longer existed.

At the beginning of the war all suffragettes were released from prison. After their work for the cause, they knew they were able women and were eager to help in the war effort. At first the government did not want to use women workers but as more and more men went off to war, women entered heavy industry in large numbers.

They worked in iron, steel, and chemical factories producing shells, bullets and other equipment for the army. It was hard and often dangerous work. Employers were suspicious of women workers but within a short while it was obvious that women were just as skilled as men.

Nearly half a million women went into industry. Others went into the Civil Service, banks and businesses. Women also worked as drivers, plumbers, engineers, porters,

During the First World War, women worked in munitions factories. Their contribution to the war effort was invaluable.

THE WAR WORKERS.
"WHAT'S ALL THIS CACKLE ABOUT VOTES AND A NEW REGISTER?"
"DON'T KNOW—OR CARE. WE'RE ALL TOO BUSY JUST NOW."

With the outbreak of the First World War, the militant suffragette movement came to an end. This cartoon shows the feeling of some suffragettes.

During the war, women were called to 'take the place of men'. The cries about the importance of a mother looking after her children were conveniently forgotten.

electricians, van drivers and bus conductresses. They did all the jobs considered unsuitable for women. They also worked as nurses, and in the army as cooks and drivers.

For many women the war brought a new independence, and higher wages than they had ever known. After the war most of them were to be pushed back into the home again. But their contribution as women was finally recognized and praised.

29

THE VOTE WON!

At the end of the war the question of votes for women was raised again. The government wanted to give the vote to soldiers and was asked whether they would also give the vote to women who had been invaluable in serving their country.

A big, peaceful women's suffrage march was again held in London and the matter was debated in the House of Commons.

Finally a decision was made. This time it was favourable. The vote was to be given to women over 30 who were householders or the wives of householders. The Act was passed in February 1918 and with it more than 8,400,000 women gained the vote. A second Act passed in the same year allowed women over 21 to become Members of Parliament. Ten years later, in 1928, the vote was extended to all women over 21. The years of fighting were over.

Suffragettes vote for the first time.

GLOSSARY

Canvassing Going from door to door, asking people to support you.
Conventions Unwritten rules of behaviour which most people accept.
Dependent To rely on another person, particularly for financial support.
Elected Chosen by vote.
House of Commons The lower chamber of Parliament, which has the power to make Britain's laws.
Independent Free from the control and support, especially financial, of others.
Industrialization The development of industry towards mechanization.
Liberal government The Liberal Party formed a strong government in 1906, holding over 400 seats in the House of Commons. They were a party committed to reform and gained victory again in 1910, but they still did not grant women the right to vote.
Martyr A person who suffers greatly, or even dies, for a cause or belief.
Opportunities Good prospects and circumstances.
Parliament A group of people elected to make the laws for the country. In Britain, this consists of the House of Commons, the House of Lords and the sovereign.
Peeresses Women holding the rank of a peer, (ie. a member of the nobility).
Political prisoners People who are in prison for their political beliefs and conscience.
Procession An orderly line of people moving along in a ceremonial manner.
Soap box A makeshift stand for a speaker who is airing his/her view in the street.
Suffragettes Members of the WSPU – a union of women who used more radical means to try and gain women the right to vote.
Suffragists People who believed in giving the vote to women, but tried through more conventional means.
Trade union A union of workers formed to negotiate with the employer for better working conditions and pay.
Truce An agreement to end fighting or a dispute.

MORE BOOKS TO READ

Non-fiction for younger readers
Kramer, Ann, *Women and Politics* (Wayland, 1988)
Ross, Stewart, *Elections* (Wayland, 1987)
Snellgrove, L.E., *Suffragettes and Votes for Women* (Longman, 1984)

Non-fiction for older readers
Mitchell, Hannah, *The Hard Way Up* (Virago, 1977)
Pankhurst, Sylvia, *The Suffragette Movement* (Virago, 1977)
Strachey, Ray, *The Cause* (Virago, 1978)

INDEX

Asquith, Prime Minister 10
Awards 25, 27

'Black Friday' 25

Canvassing 24
'Cat and Mouse Act' 15, 24
'Cause, the' 9, 12, 25, 26, 28
Clements Inn headquarters
   8, 26
Clothes and appearance 4,
   13, 14, 22–23

Davison, Emily 25
Derby Day tragedy 25
Downing Street 10

Elections 4, 6, 30

Family life 17
First World War 28
Force feeding 15, 25
Friendship and
   companionship 27

Hardship and suffering 5
Health and sickness 24, 25

Heckling 10, 14, 27
Home life 7, 18–19
House of Commons 7, 30

Imprisonment and arrest 10
Independence 17, 29

Job opportunities 16, 17

Kenney, Annie 10, 20

Liberal government 10, 15

Marches and meetings
   12–13, 23, 27, 30
Marriage 16–17
Members of Parliament 6,
   7, 30
Mill workers 9, 20
Mitchell, Hannah 17
'Mouse Castle' 24
Munitions factories 28

Newspapers 5, 10, 11, 13

Parliament 4, 6, 7, 10
Pankhurst, Christabel 8, 10
Pankhurst, Emmeline 8, 28
Pankhurst, Sylvia 5, 24
Police, the 10, 11, 24, 25

Prison 14–15, 24, 25, 28
Public meetings 4, 5, 10

Recreation and pastimes
   26–27

Suffrage, women's 4, 5, 6, 7,
   10, 30
Suffragettes 5, 10
   middle-class 7, 9, 18
   working-class 9, 18, 19

Tactics and militant actions
   10–11, 19, 28
Trade Unions 19

Victoria, Queen 7
'Votes for Women'
   newspaper 12

War effort, the 28–29
Window smashing 11
Winning the vote 30
Women's Social and
   Poltical Union (WSPU)
   8, 9, 16, 23, 26, 28
Work 18, 20–21

Picture acknowledgements

The pictures in this book were supplied by the following: Ann Ronan Picture Library 7 (below), 29 (left); Barnaby's Picture Library 10; BBC Hulton Picture Library 17, 18 (right), 20 (right), 21 (right), 28; BPCC/Aldus Archive 18 (left); The Bridgeman Art Library 6 (left), 11 (left); ET Archives 6 (right), 27 (below); The Mansell Collection 7 (above), 9 (left), 13, 23 (above); Mary Evans Picture Library 5, 8, 9 (far left), 9 (right), 12 (both), 15 (left), 25 (left), 26, 27 (above); Picturepoint 15 (right), 16 (right); Popperfoto 19, 25 (both); TOPHAM 16 (left), 20 (left), 21 (left), 23 (left), 29 (right).